CLUES TO AMERICAN FURNITURE

CLUES
to
American
Furniture

Revised Edition

By Jean Taylor Federico
Illustrated by Judith Curcio

STARRHILL PRESS
Washington, D.C.

For Happy and her Best Friend

Published by Starrhill Press
P.O. Box 21038
Washington, DC 20009-0538

Library of Congress Cataloging in Publication Data

Federico, Jean Taylor, 1940
     Clues to American furniture / Jean Taylor Federico ;
  illustrated by Judith Curcio. — Rev. ed.
        p.   cm.
  Includes bibliographical references.
  ISBN 0-913515-75-2 : $7.95
     1. Furniture—United States—Styles. I. Curcio, Judith.
  II. Title.
  NK2405.F43   1991
  749.213'075—dc20   91-25233
                                                    CIP

Printed in the United States of America

First edition, 1988; revised edition, 1991

3 5 7 6 4

Introduction 7

17th Century:
17th Century/Pilgrim 8

18th Century:
Early 18th Century/William and Mary 12
Baroque/Queen Anne 16
Rococo/Chippendale 22

Late 18th and Early 19th Centuries:
Neoclassical/Federal 30
Neoclassical/Empire 36

Country, Windsor and Folk: 42

The Victorian Age:
Gothic Revival 48
Rococo Revival 49
Renaissance Revival 50
Eastlake Style 50
Colonial Revival 51
Wicker 52

Precursors to the 20th Century:
Bentwood 53
Art Nouveau 53
The Arts and Crafts Movement 54
Mission Style 54
Prairie School 55
Art Deco 56

20th Century:
International Style 57
Artists/Craftsmen 61

Furniture Collections to Visit 65

Suggested Reading 69

Index 70

Terms and Dates of Furniture Styles

Term Used in This Book	Style Dates	Traditional Term
17th Century	1650-1690	Pilgrim
Early 18th Century	1690-1730	William and Mary
Baroque	1725-1750	Queen Anne
Rococo	1750-1790	Chippendale
Neoclassical I	1790-1815	Federal
Neoclassical II	1815-1840	Empire
Country	1650-	
Windsor	1760-	
Folk	18th & 19th c.	
Gothic Revival	1840-1880	Victorian
Rococo Revival	1840-1870	Victorian
Renaissance Revival	1850-1880	Victorian
Eastlake Style	1870-1890	
Colonial Revival	1876-1925	
Wicker	1885-1925	
Bentwood	1870-1930	
Art Nouveau	1895-1915	
Arts and Crafts	1880-1915	
Mission Style	1890-1915	
Prairie School	1895-1915	
Art Deco	1918-1939	
International Style	1915-	
Artists/Craftsmen	1945-	

This illustrated guide book introduces the pertinent terms used in the study of American furniture and includes illustrations of pieces from each major style period. The book treats furniture made in America from the 17th century to the present time with line drawings of period rooms, characteristic pieces and details. These provide clear clues to stylistic differences which in turn enable one to experience the joy of recognizing the period of a particular piece of furniture and of giving it a name.

Traditional names of styles of American furniture have been dictated by a variety of circumstances and have led to great confusion. Most names in common use today were never used during the period and refer to reigns of monarchs, emperors, or trend setters rather than to the style itself. Often the names are anachronistic. For these reasons I have suggested alternate terms which are descriptive of the style and appropriate here, without being concerned about periods of political dominance by one monarch or another. The brief chart on the opposite page will aid in clarifying the various periods, styles and dates. One must remember that dates for styles are approximate and that styles do overlap.

Readers may question the inclusion of the International style in a book which discusses the history of American furniture. But just as styles in the mid-18th century were strongly influenced by the designs of Thomas Chippendale, who never set foot in this country, so too, much of our 20th-century furniture design is dominated by noted international artists. It is significant that design today continues to reveal a desire for personal expression executed not in the factory but by individual craftspeople, and that there also continues to be a role for the artisan/craftsman who can provide new interpretations for individual patrons.

For many this book will be a quick, easy reference; for others, an introduction to the most salient and distinctive features of American furniture styles. For all, it is meant to further one's enjoyment of the arts and to provide an opportunity to test one's eye when looking at the rich and varied styles of furniture made in America.

Jean Taylor Federico

*A 17th-Century Room
in New England*

Furniture made by the earliest colonists, who tended to emigrate from rural England rather than from London, shows strong similarities in design and technique to the vernacular English furniture of the time. It was sturdy and practical, constructed of solid wood, primarily oak and pine, and consisted mainly of chests, beds, tables, stools and benches. Chairs were a scarce item in most homes.

Furniture of the 17th century was not made in isolation by unskilled craftsmen. By the 1630s, residents of Boston and Salem had the advantages of wealth and trade with England. Emigrating artisans brought with them the latest designs and construction techniques from London.

One of the earliest known American-made chairs is the Wainscot chair, made of oak and modeled on English 16th-century furniture. Today "Wainscot chair" describes a form of seating furniture made of solid pieces of wood with arms and a back which can be unadorned or elaborately carved.

Furniture makers of the 17th century called themselves "joiners." The simplest way to join furniture components was the nailed butt joint. "Board chests" were quickly made by nailing wide boards together and placing a lid on top. Joiners also used the familiar mortise-and-tenon joint, but only the very few who had emigrated from London or the Continent could do dovetail joints.

The carver and the "turner," who turned wood on a lathe, provided decoration on some early pieces, notably dower chests from the Connecticut River Valley; the use of applied split spindles is seen on furniture from Salem and Essex County in Massachusetts. Split spindles are made by carefully splitting a piece of wood, gluing the two pieces back together, turning the glued piece on a lathe and then resplitting it to form two perfectly matched pieces, which are then applied to a chest. Designs were painted on some furniture of this period. Turners also repaired broken chairs and made seating furniture, dishes, utensils and tool handles from wood.

This style is also called "Jacobean," from the Latin name for James I of

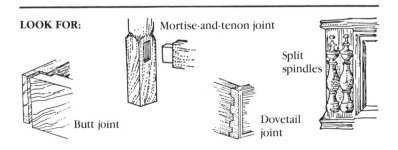

LOOK FOR:

Butt joint

Mortise-and-tenon joint

Split spindles

Dovetail joint

England (1603-1625). Most recently, it has been termed "mannerist," relating it to its European influences. Decoration on American 17th-century furniture can be traced back to Dutch print sources from about 1480, when Roman ruins with intense decoration, often in geometric patterns, were rediscovered. "Mannerist" derives from the Italian *maniera,* meaning "grace" in the 16th century.

Although 17th-century furniture is closely associated with New England, a few pieces made in the South are in existence.

Side chair,
Rhode Island

Joint stool

Court cupboard

Armchair with
turned decoration

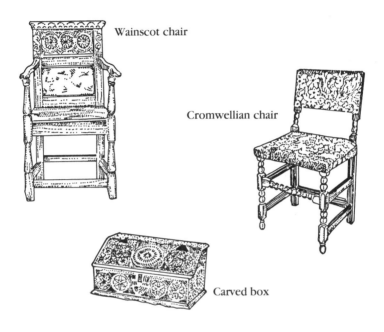

Wainscot chair

Cromwellian chair

Carved box

Dower chest,
Connecticut River Valley

Dower chest,
Hadley, Massachusetts

MARY · BVRT

*A Room in the William and Mary
or Early 18th-Century Style*

William and Mary, in their move from the Dutch to the English throne, took with them a number of Dutch and Huguenot artisans. The combination of Dutch and French ideas created unusual design elements in early 18th-century English furniture, most notably elaborate baroque carving and turning. At the same time a busy trade with the Far East brought from China such innovations as the use of caning and curved backs in seating furniture.

A growing trade between London and the American colonies served to heighten interest in the fashions of England and the Continent. Increased immigration inevitably brought to the colonies more skilled artisans who were able to execute new furniture designs. Often called "William and Mary," the style is still very closely tied to that of the late 17th-century. However, it was produced by a distinct group of professional artisans commissioned for specific and wealthy clients.

Early 18th-century furniture is characterized by straight, angular lines interrupted by multiple turnings. It is also distinguished by a wide variety of new forms such as gate-leg tables, chests of drawers, high chests, desks and looking glasses.

It was during this period that the easy or "wing" chair first appeared. This was an exceedingly expensive chair as it was upholstered, usually in a fine fabric. Not only was this chair more comfortable than the hard, straight-backed Wainscot and Cromwellian chairs, but it had the distinct advantage, in an era before central heating, of warding off drafts.

It was in these years that the craft specialist emerged. No longer was a chair wholly constructed by one craftsman: now the turner shaped the trumpets, vases and balls found on legs and stretchers, a carver fashioned the ornaments on the tops of the chair backs, the joiner assembled and glued the pieces, and for the first time, the upholsterer assumed a prominent role.

An attractive feature of furniture made in this period was the use of decorative veneer to highlight the natural colors and designs in the graining of the wood.

LOOK FOR:

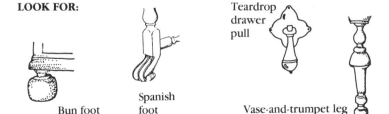

Bun foot

Spanish foot

Teardrop drawer pull

Vase-and-trumpet leg

Easy chair

Gateleg table

Desk

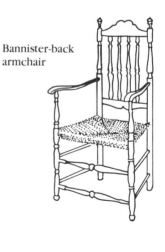

Bannister-back
armchair

Dressing table

Cane-seated
side chair

Day-bed

Painted blanket chest

Chest-on-frame

A Room in the
Baroque or Queen Anne Style

The gracefully balanced, unadorned curve of the Queen Anne style, which dominated American furniture design from about 1725 to 1750, continues to please the 20th-century eye. It is interesting to note that Queen Anne, who reigned in England from 1702 to 1714, had little, if anything, to do with any style of decorative arts. Queen Anne furniture was first labeled such in the late 19th century. A more appropriate title for this decorative style would be "Baroque."

The gently curved lines of the Queen Anne style are in clear contrast to the tight turning and straight, often angular, lines of the earlier William and Mary period. The major style marking of this period is the cabriole leg. The word *cabriole,* meaning "hind leg of a goat," hardly conveys the elegance of this S-shaped leg which was to dominate furniture design through much of the 18th century. The S-curve is echoed in the graceful line of the crest rail at the top of the chair, and again in its vase-form splat.

A penchant for things Chinese was apparent throughout the century, particularly reflected in the fashion for drinking tea in appropriate porcelain bowls and cups. It is not surprising to find tea tables in vogue during this period.

The imitation of the processes and motifs of Chinese decorative art, known as *chinoiserie,* produced several new design elements. *Japanning,* a decorative process that simulated Oriental lacquer work, was used on very expensive furniture of the period, particularly in Boston. First a chalk-like material, not unlike gesso, was applied to the front of the piece of furniture, covering the locally available pine or maple. A dark color, made from vermilion and lampblack and giving the appearance of tortoise shell, was then applied. On this background Oriental figures and mythic creatures were painted. Sometimes the figures were raised and three-dimensional; sometimes gold leaf and metallic dust were used. The effect was one of great beauty when the furniture form itself had been constructed with pleasing proportions and graceful lines.

LOOK FOR:

Butterfly
drawer pull

Baroque
crest rails
and vase splats

Carved
baroque
shell

Some suggest that the Oriental influence is seen most clearly in the adaptation of the claw of a Chinese dragon, grasping out toward a pearl, in the ball-and-claw foot found often in French and English furniture of this period. In American Baroque furniture, the pad foot is dominant, with the ball-and-claw foot appearing only occasionally in New York pieces. In the Chippendale style, which follows, the ball-and-claw foot becomes a major style marking.

The entire 18th century is one of pervasive order, proportion and dimension. (We often fail to appreciate the dominance of the classic order as early as the Queen Anne period and find erroneously that Neoclassicism seemed to invent the return to classicism.) All furniture forms, particularly large case pieces such as high chests, can be analyzed in relation to their maker's understanding of proportion. Some of these relationships were complex, but the trained architect or furniture designer was always well grounded in his study of the Roman architect, Vitruvius. Because of Vitruvius's mathematical, classical interpretation which we can place on furniture of this period, it becomes easy, with a bit of training, to recognize problems in case pieces. For example, the usual height of a low chest or dressing table is 30″. The usual height of the base for a high chest is 36″. "Married" pieces (those that have been assembled at a later date) often lose this proportion, especially when the marriage is made with a dressing table, which is always lower in height.

Cabinetmakers of this period continued to use the wood of native walnut and maple trees. Only occasionally did a wealthy client order pieces in imported mahogany. The addition of carved shells or leaves also added considerably to the price. It is uncommon to find veneering on American Baroque furniture.

Although the fine Queen Anne furniture made in Philadelphia, Boston and Newport has been more frequently illustrated and written about, some of the finest examples of this style were made in Charleston, South Carolina.

LOOK FOR:

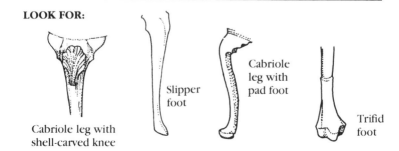

Cabriole leg with shell-carved knee

Slipper foot

Cabriole leg with pad foot

Trifid foot

Armchair with
upholstered seat,
Philadelphia

Side chair
with stretchers,
New England

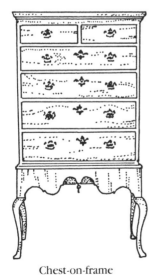

Chest-on-frame

Looking
glass

Low chest or
dressing table

Dressing table,
Charleston

Desk-on-frame

High chest
with flat top

Tilt-top tea table
with bird-cage
support

Drop-leaf
dining table

Tea table

Card table

High chest
with bonnet top

A Room in the
Rococo or Chippendale Style

The middle of the 1700s found the colonies maturing culturally as well as economically and politically. However, they still looked to England and Europe as style centers for the arts.

With the London publication in 1754 of *The Gentlemen and Cabinet Maker's Director*, by Thomas Chippendale, a new style of furniture was fully described. Chippendale was not himself an innovator, but his meticulous drawings clearly documented the major style sentiments of London. The catalogue was immensely popular and served to influence craftsmen in America as well as designers and decorators in England. Several design influences, particularly Chinese, Gothic and Rococo, can be recognized both in Chippendale's drawings and in American furniture of the period.

Although Thomas Chippendale never made furniture for American clients, and only a few American cabinetmakers might have actually owned copies of the *Director,* the style spread to the colonies with English craftsmen who emigrated and brought it with them. Newspaper advertisements of the period, always a good resource for decorative arts historians, often describe a merchant or craftsman as being "late of London" or his wares as being "in the newest and latest style." Another way the style spread, perhaps more significantly than the effect of the design book itself, was by those few pieces of furniture made in London in the Chippendale style that were shipped to America and became prototypes for colonial craftsmen.

The changes from the Queen Anne or Baroque style to the Rococo were not so much in form as in ornamentation. The graceful curve of the Queen Anne chair became more pronounced, almost angular; the crest rail, gently curved in the former style, gained ears and additional scrolling; the plain splat of the Queen Anne chair was transformed into a

LOOK FOR:

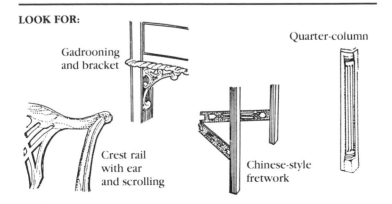

Gadrooning and bracket

Quarter-column

Crest rail with ear and scrolling

Chinese-style fretwork

sculptural tour de force by the carvers. In the 18th century, a cabinet maker might have used the term "pierced bannister" for what we call today a carved splat. A bonnet-topped high chest with ball-and-claw feet was described as having "crown and claws."

By the mid-19th century, the name Chippendale had become the term associated with American furniture made in the latter half of the 1700s. Had other designers such as Manwaring, Ince or Mayhew been better known, this style might have had another name. Today the term "Rococo," which actually describes the style, seems more appropriate. The word is derived from the French *rocaille* meaning rock or grotto work and well expresses the sculptural, ornately carved shells, leaves and scroll forms that appear on many of the decorated pieces.

From approximately 1750 to 1790, the Rococo style flourished in the major colonial cities and towns: Boston, Newport, New York, Philadelphia, Baltimore, Annapolis, Williamsburg and Charleston. Situated on major trading routes with England, these cities were readily exposed to the latest styles from abroad, and it was in and around these urban seaports that the wealthy clients lived. The new merchant class created the market.

Both furniture makers and carvers learned their trades as apprentices. There was relatively little movement by these trained artisans—they tended to learn under one master and then later to develop their own clientele in the same area. Furniture was custom-ordered, and the amount of carving on the knees, splat and crest rail was a question of economics. Chairs were usually bought in sets; the price of a set of furniture increased in proportion to the time required by the carver to decorate each piece. It is important to note that less decorated furniture did not, per se, mean a new design or a transition from one style to the next; rather it indicated a cost-conscious client.

Regional characteristics are easily discernible on furniture made in the Rococo style. In Newport, Rhode Island, for example, the wealthy, conservative clientele preferred the carved, symmetrical shell decoration

Drawer pulls

Cartouche, from top of high chest

Carved rococo shell

Rosette and finial

which had been popular a generation earlier. In Boston, sharp facades and angular shapes were emphasized; there was a preference for the bombé shape and block-fronting in desks, secretary bookcases and chests; and carving and decoration, the major characteristics of the Rococo style, tended to be restrained and less well-defined. By comparison, the furniture made in Philadelphia, where both the clientele and the craftsmen fully understood and appreciated the designs featured in Chippendale's *Director,* was among the most highly decorated and carefully carved. Philadelphia was by this time the major center of style and wealth in the colonies. Design books were more readily available and hence more influential, and craftsmen were not only more numerous but also more skilled. In addition, the wealthy clientele tended to support and purchase from those craftsmen who produced objects in the the newest and latest styles.

Construction techniques provide further clues to the origin of a piece. Many New England chairs, for example, were constructed with stretchers to provide stability, while Philadelphia craftsmen preferred to employ a through-tenon to stabilize the joining of the side seat rail to the back. The inside construction of a seat or the method of forming the leg and knee become clues for the advanced student.

Microscopic analysis of secondary wood used for interior construction of case pieces and seating furniture can also reveal where a piece was made. While the visible exterior wood of a high-style piece was usually walnut or imported mahogany, or maple or cherry in New England, cabinetmakers used inexpensive local wood—cypress in South Carolina, yellow pine in Virginia, and tulip poplar around Baltimore—for what could not be seen.

Regional characteristics in furniture styles were fading by the mid-19th century as machines supplanted the individual craftsman. Conservative styles tended to endure longer in remote areas, and the term, "country Chippendale," is used to describe furniture of a simple, highly vernacular craftsmanship that may have been made as late as 1810.

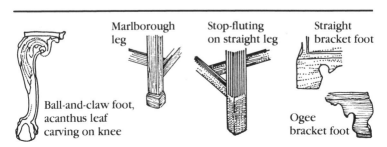

Ball-and-claw foot, acanthus leaf carving on knee

Marlborough leg

Stop-fluting on straight leg

Straight bracket foot

Ogee bracket foot

Upholstered open armchair, or elbow chair

Side chair, Virginia

Tea table

Tall case clock

Chest-on-chest

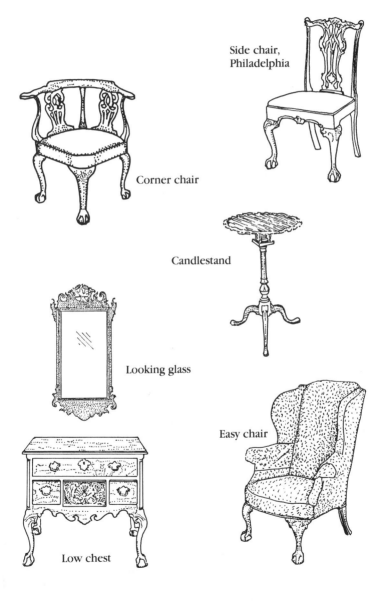

Side chair, Philadelphia

Corner chair

Candlestand

Looking glass

Easy chair

Low chest

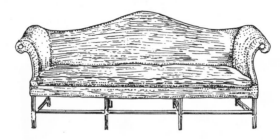

Camel-back sofa

Pembroke table

Bombé chest
of drawers

Serpentine-front
chest of drawers

Block-front
chest of drawers,
New England

Card table

Card table

Slant-top desk

Chest-on-frame

High chest
with bonnet top

A Dining Room in the
Early Neoclassical or Federal Style

The Neoclassical style in American decorative arts can be seen in objects made from about 1785 to 1840. Many divide this era into the Federal period (approximately 1785-1815) and the Empire period (1815-1840). While the first nicely fits a discussion of the new republic and the second refers directly to the era of the Napoleonic Empire, these terms in no way describe the style itself. At the time, it was referred to as the "antique taste," and we prefer the comparable term "Neoclassical" to describe both early and late phases of the style.

The spirit and vigor that accompanied the move from colonial status to that of independent nation called for change in all facets of American life including the decorative arts. By the 1780s, the imagination of Europe's culturally elite had been fired by the archaeological discoveries at Herculaneum and Pompeii. Decorators, designers, architects, and historians had all made the grand tour to Italy, and many designers had returned home to transform the houses of the wealthy into the classical look. By the 1770s, in England and on the Continent, the elegant new style was evident everywhere—in draperies, classical borders, swags, urns, vases, and inlay-decorated furniture.

By the late 1780s, this "antique taste" was influencing design in America as well. The delicacy and restraint of the new style was in sharp contrast to the robust carving of rococo leaves and shells of pre Revolution American furniture. A sense of contour was achieved by the use of inlays and relatively flat carving. Legs were thin and formed straight lines, nearly devoid of three-dimensional qualities. Feet were merely the end of a very thin leg. Instead of the curved crest rails of Baroque and Rococo furniture, chairs were now straight, angular or squared off. Shapes with classical figures, usually a vase or an urn, formed the splat. Shield-back chairs were popular. All forms of decoration appeared more molded than carved.

Inlay, which appeals to the eye because of its juxtaposition of different colors, was the major decorative innovation of the period. The region where a particular piece of Federal furniture was made can often be determined by the shapes of its inlay work: bellflowers made in Baltimore differ from bellflowers made in Boston.

LOOK FOR:

Drawer pull

Eglomisé panel in looking glass

Shield-back chair back

The interest in two-dimensional ornamentation revived another decorative system—the use of veneer. Solid mahogany was expensive; a thin layer of mahogany, glued onto less costly wood, was far more economical. Moreover, veneer could be easily manipulated around the graceful turns on the fronts of card tables and other pieces.

New centers of furniture craftsmanship developed in the young nation. Furniture made in the bustling town of Baltimore caught the public fancy with its carefully executed classical images painted by Baltimore artisans on splats and chair backs, some actually depicting well-known buildings. The use of églomisé panels (reverse painting on glass) was another characteristic of Baltimore pieces. And inlay makers were creating a variety of decorations inspired by classical motifs as well as delicate vines and airy flowers. Baltimore craftsmen also made shield-back chairs and the full complement of new forms found in this style. Working with locally available support wood, usually tulip poplar, they made tasteful furniture that appealed to a growing population.

Major designers of the first neoclassical period were England's Adam brothers, George Hepplewhite, Thomas Sheraton, Thomas Hope and Thomas Shearer. Both Hepplewhite and Sheraton printed design books which were popular in America. Today, many use their names as terms for styles: "Hepplewhite" to describe a chair with a square tapered leg and an oval or shield back, "Sheraton" to describe one with a round, but reeded, tapered leg with small columns on the sides of a squared back. In actual fact, each man illustrated both styles in his design book. The use of these two designers' names is today both unnecessary and confusing.

The delicacy of the first phase of American Neoclassical design was a quality not often expressed in the English prototypes. Some feel that this was America's first true design style, for while it owed much to its English and French cousins, the interpretation was purely American.

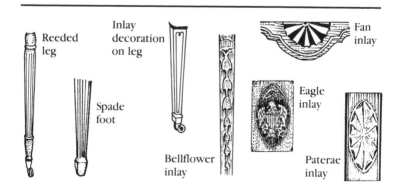

Reeded leg

Inlay decoration on leg

Spade foot

Bellflower inlay

Fan inlay

Eagle inlay

Paterae inlay

Shield-back
armchair

Armchair with
urn-shaped splat

Side chair

Lady's
work table

Settee with painted decoration, Baltimore

Inlaid serpentine
sideboard

Candlestand

Desk and bookcase

Bed frame,
Salem, Massachusetts

Inlaid card table

Side table

Three-part dining table,
Maryland

Lady's writing desk
with églomisé decoration

Writing desk,
tambour front

A Parlor in the
Late Neoclassical or Empire Style

The second phase of the Neoclassical style was still inspired by the glories of Rome and of Greece, but it had a distinct French accent. The forms became heavier, the shapes bolder, the carving robustly three-dimensional, and the decorative elements positively flamboyant. Mounted ormolu (stamped, gold-plated brass imported from France), strongly contrasting colors, painting, stenciling, gilding, marble and alabaster all found a place in this ornate, early 19th-century style.

The difference between the two Neoclassical styles can be understood by looking at silver produced during the two periods. The major decoration of earlier silver pieces was engraving or "bright cutting," a two-dimensional decoration only visible on close study. In the later period, the forms were the same only larger, embossed rather than engraved, and often heavy with applied, three-dimensional decoration. In like manner, the delicate inlay work incised into the wood of early Neoclassical pieces was supplanted by the bold, high-relief carving of later pieces.

In furniture of this period, the influence of French craftsmen is apparent, especially that of Charles Honoré Lannuier, an émigré who fled to this country shortly after the French Revolution. He brought with him a familiarity with the French Empire style, the mounting of ormolu, and the technique of elaborate veneering in rich, figured mahogany.

European design books illustrating Empire designs were generally available in America by 1815 and further popularized the style. A highly favored English publication was Rudolph Ackermann's *Repository of the Arts*, whose colored illustrations were accompanied by sample fabric swatches. From France came *Recueil des décorations intérieures*, by Charles Percier and P.F.L. Fontaine. These two designers put forth the notion that a room's furnishings should reflect its interior architectural detailing which, conforming to the Greek Revival architecture of the period, was ordered, symmetrical and balanced.

This concept, echoed by many high-style designers, generated several new furniture forms, notably Grecian sofas, sleigh beds, pier tables and

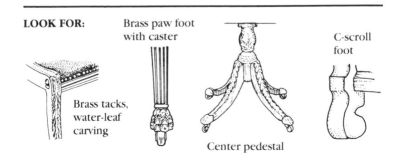

LOOK FOR:

Brass paw foot with caster

Brass tacks, water-leaf carving

Center pedestal

C-scroll foot

the center table. Pier tables, usually with a mirror at the back of the base, were made to fit between windows in the parlor and were often purchased in pairs to stand on opposite walls. Similarly, sofas were bought in pairs and placed facing each other, perhaps with a marble-topped center table between them. Furniture pieces were no longer light enough to move easily around a room, and so they were equipped with casters.

It has been suggested that furniture made in this late phase shows a "more correct" classical interpretation than that of the earlier period. Some chairs made in Baltimore and New York had a "klismos" leg, an element borrowed from classical friezes. The lyre and the female head were similarly adopted. Craftsmen referred to "Roman feet" on card tables which, in Baltimore, were painted in "Pompeiian red." Reeding, based on early Roman decoration and introduced during the earlier phase, became more prominent. Egyptian motifs included winged figures as well as carved lotus and water leaves, the latter usually found on legs.

Instead of waiting for pieces to be ordered individually, craftsmen began to build up stocks of furniture in warehouses. With the introduction of the circular saw, production methods improved and furniture of widely varying quality and price could be offered to a growing middle-class. The numbers of customers and the size of their orders persuaded furniture makers to develop companies to deal with the demand. One of the most successful of these was established in New York by a Scottish immigrant named Duncan Phyfe. Phyfe, one of America's best known furniture makers, employed as many as 100 craftsmen to produce his distinctive, richly grained, classical pieces in both solid and veneered mahogany.

As mechanization took hold of American industry in the mid-19th century, reduced production costs brought high-style furniture within reach of many instead of just a favored few.

Sculptural
carving and
fruit basket

Prince
of Wales
feathers

Stenciled
decoration

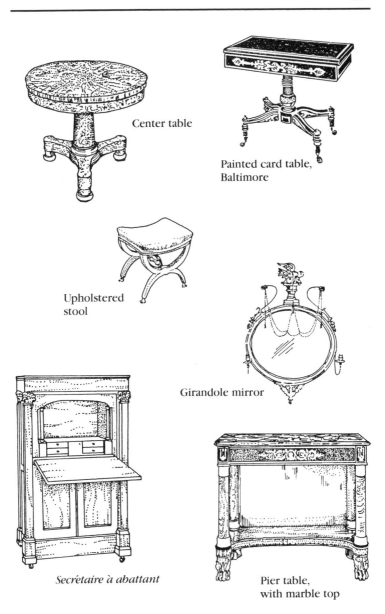

Center table

Painted card table,
Baltimore

Upholstered
stool

Girandole mirror

Secrétaire à abattant

Pier table,
with marble top

Lyre-back
side chair

Painted side chair,
klismos type,
Philadelphia

Two-part dining table

Card table

Sideboard

Lady's work table

Side chair,
Duncan Phyfe

Cane-seated
side chair,
Duncan Phyfe

Sofa, Samuel McIntire,
Salem, Massachusetts

Painted settee, Philadelphia

A 19th-Century German Room in Texas

Up to this point, we have discussed high style furniture, made for a select few, often on special order. During the same period, furniture was being made in small towns and country areas using some of the style characteristics of the sophisticated urban pieces but without the same consistency of proportion, detailing and woods. Today we call this "country" furniture. Rather than imported wood, we see considerable use of local maple, pine, cherry and walnut, with seats of woven flag or rush. The tendency of styles to endure much longer in rural regions makes accurate dating of country pieces difficult.

Inventory records show that 18th-and early 19th-century Americans, farmer and merchant alike, purchased Windsor chairs by the dozens. Windsor chairs found places in almost every American home. Although today we prefer our furniture in its natural wood tone, 18th- and 19th-century chairs were painted—in red, dark green, black or brown—to give a consistent color to the wide variety of local woods used in the making of these chairs.

By the beginning of the 19th century, relatively inexpensive seating furniture was being manufactured in Philadelphia, New York, Baltimore, Norfolk and Alexandria. Perhaps the most popular was the "fancy" chair—a painted, highly decorated side chair with rush or cane seating. Standard-sized legs and rungs made production quick and cheap. Lambert Hitchcock began producing these chairs in the early 19th century in Connecticut; "Hitchcock chair" has become an almost generic term for this style.

The functional simplicity of Shaker furniture has captured the imagination of today's collectors. Furniture crafted at Shaker communities in New England, New York State, Ohio and Kentucky reflect an honoring of order and craftsmanship. Shaker furniture was made either for the community (the Believers) or for others (the World). Rocking chairs were an especially popular form which Shaker communities sold to the World.

Noteworthy among immigrant groups whose folk traditions have contributed much to American art forms are the Pennsylvania Germans who came to America in the 18th century. Brightly painted stylized animals, trees and flowers were applied to available woods—walnut, oak, pine and tulip poplar—in such forms as dower chests, cupboards and wardrobes. Pieces were massive by today's standard: a large "shrank" or wardrobe was often constructed so that it could be taken apart for moving.

Some furniture pieces made in German-settled areas of Texas are particularly sought after today. Made from the 1830s to the 1880s, these pieces show the influence of the Biedermeier style (a sort of low-style Empire design).

Most of our earlier scholarship has focused on the decorative arts of the Anglo-American tradition. Only recently have we begun to reevaluate contributions made by other cultures, especially those who settled in more remote areas of this country. Spanish colonists brought with them traditions of design and craftsmanship, which can still be seen in furniture made in New Mexico in the early 19th century. Most examples are made of pine and decorated with surface carving, paint and sometimes cutout designs. The recent rediscovery of Spanish colonial architecture and furniture has made the "Southwestern look" a popular style with true historical antecedents.

Important examples of French colonial furniture were made throughout New France, particularly along the Mississippi River from New Orleans to St. Louis. This French colonial style is decidedly different from the French highstyle of the neoclassical period when major designers such as Charles Honoré Lannuier emigrated to New York.

As we study and analyze more carefully, we will no doubt come to appreciate more fully the contributions of Africans, both slave and free, to the furniture-making tradition in America. We are already seeing the influences of African design, color and techniques in the production of American textiles and woven baskets.

Pie safe

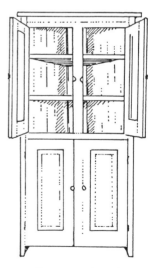

Corner cupboard

Jelly cupboard

Rustic or
Adirondack
armchair,
New York State

Painted
side chair

Ladder-back
side chair,
rush seat

Country
Chippendale
side chair,
Connecticut
River Valley

Country
Chippendale
side chair,
painted
decoration

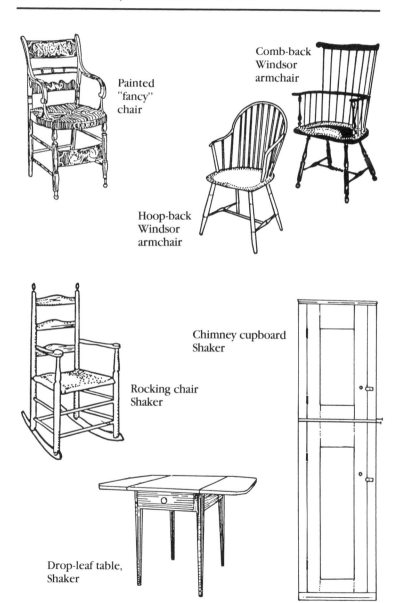

Painted
"fancy"
chair

Comb-back
Windsor
armchair

Hoop-back
Windsor
armchair

Chimney cupboard
Shaker

Rocking chair
Shaker

Drop-leaf table,
Shaker

Plank chair,
Ohio

Painted schrank,
Pennsylvania German

Table
New Mexico, early 19th century

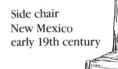

Side chair
New Mexico
early 19th century

Armoire
New Orleans
early 19th century

Table
New Orleans
early 18th century

The use of the term "Victorian furniture" cannot begin to describe the variety of styles that appeared in American homes from about 1840 through the end of the 19th century. This was a period of eclectic tastes which could be gratified relatively inexpensively. During the Industrial Revolution, machines quickly replaced the individual craftsman of earlier generations, reducing the cost of furniture manufacture, and bringing the cost of large sets of furniture within reach of many people. We also see larger, bolder individual pieces being made, and the widespread use of laminated woods that were pressed and then carved into intricate designs.

Gothic Revival: 1840-1880

Although Thomas Chippendale had used the term "gothic" in his *Director*, the name of this Victorian revival style probably owes more to the popularity of romantic "gothic" novels by such writers as Sir Walter Scott and to a general preoccupation with the Middle Ages. Andrew Jackson Downing presented several major concepts about the gothic style in his book, *The Architecture of Country Houses*. To identify Gothic Revival furniture, one should look for rosewood and dark varnish. Oak was also popular as it evoked the Middle Ages. The decorative forms included the Gothic arch, carved trefoils, quatrefoils, spool and ball turnings. Some chair backs even resembled rose windows.

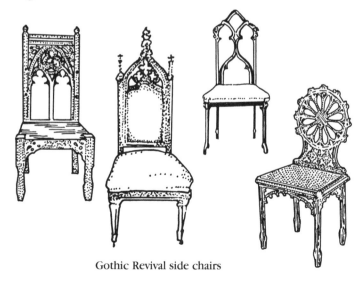

Gothic Revival side chairs

Rococo Revival: 1840-1870

This style looked back to 18th-century France for inspiration while taking full advantage of 19th-century machine technology to produce its tendrils, wreathes, hanging foliage, budding flowers, full-blown roses, grapes, vines, birds and scrolls. Called "Louis Quatorze" at the time, in actual fact it approached more closely the style of Louis XV. Some of the forms themselves carry French names: méridienne (a shortened, one-armed sofa), and étagère (a bookcase or "whatnot shelf" for holding the variety of objects collected by the Victorians). Large parlor groupings were sold, consisting of seven pieces: an arm chair, a lady's chair, a sofa and four smaller parlor chairs. There might have been a center table as well. Laminated rosewood, marble-covered surfaces, horsehair upholstery and highly decorated, gilded mirrors, overmantles and pier glasses were popular.

The cabinetmakers Alexander Roux and Charles Baudouine, who emigrated from France, executed this style in New York primarily for the wealthy. Later, craftsmen familiar with the style emigrated from England and Germany and made Rococo Revival furniture for the middle classes. As in the century before, design books and manuals also helped bring the style to America.

The style was very popular in the South where many fine homes were decorated by New York designers and filled with furniture made by John Henry Belter and Joseph Meeks and Sons.

Rococo Revival Sofa

Renaissance Revival: 1850-1880

Renaissance Revival furniture is characteristically angular and jagged, easily distinguished from flowery Rococo Revival pieces. Early pieces in the style, showing influences from 16th-century French furniture, were made of walnut and decorated with applied or carved cartouches, animals and human figures. Ormolu (gilded brass), porcelain and marquetry (a decorative veneer of shaped pieces of wood, bone or ivory in a mosaic form) contributed to the decorative effect. A second phase is reminiscent of Louis XVI furniture with its square backs, turned and fluted legs, gilt, ebony and, again, ormolu mounts. And finally, we see the incorporation of Greek, Roman and Egyptian decorative motifs such as sphinx heads on the arms and backs of chairs and sofas. Although it is almost impossible to describe a pure form of this style, the ebullient variety of its decoration expresses the Victorian love of the unexpected and need to decorate every possible surface.

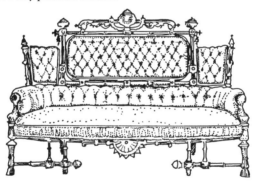

Renaissance Revival Sofa

Eastlake Style: 1870-1890

Soon all of these bizarre decorations would resolve into a simpler form—the Eastlake style. Jagged angles were squared off, and heavily applied decoration was replaced with the flat simplicity of incised decoration. Charles Eastlake, in his 1868 publication, *Hints on Household Taste,* maintained a preference for craftsmanship, simplicity and solid forms—above all, he sought to improve the taste exemplified in modern manufactured objects. (His publication offered a great deal of advice but not many illustrations for furniture design.) Custom-made furniture showing Eastlake's influence was produced by Leon Marcotte and Christian Herter in New York and by Daniel Pabst of Philadelphia. But furniture in the extraordinarily popular Eastlake style was also mass-produced in Grand Rapids, Michigan, which by the end of the century could boast sixty furniture factories.

Cane-seated side chair

Oak dresser

Colonial Revival: 1876-1925

And finally, the appearance of Colonial Revival furniture coincided with the search for our American past that was inspired by the Centennial celebrations in 1876. These "modern antiques" took their designs from early American styles, and we see reproductions of Chippendale, Queen Anne and even 17th-century pieces being made by manufacturers such as A.H. Davenport of Boston. Colonial Revival continues to be a popular furnishing style, although today we more commonly use the term "reproduction."

Wainscot-type armchair

Baroque-type armchair

Early 18th-century-type armchair

The popularity of wicker furniture in the late 19th century coincided with a heightened sense of leisure. Americans now had time to spend on their porches, and wicker was the ideal material for porch furniture. Treatises on household and domestic economy advised light, airy, "healthful" furniture, and wicker suited this concept. By the end of the 19th century, childhood for the middle and upper classes was being looked upon as a unique and special time; children came into their own, with wicker furniture to match. Wicker pieces, with removable upholstered cushions, were equally popular in the parlor or in the summer home.

This furniture, which could be left in its natural colors or painted, was made of a combination of different materials: sturdy hardwood frames were covered with combinations of rattan, cane, reed, willow, fiber, oriental seagrass, prairie grass, raffia and rush. The number of materials used in a wicker chair was matched by the variety of decoration seen in its design—curlicues and beadwork, intricate weaving, scrollwork and spider web motifs. Wicker designs were often influenced by the Orient and seemed to satisfy the consumer's desire for the exotic.

The development of specialized machinery, such as the circular loom for the weaving of the wicker, made it possible to produce wicker furniture inexpensively. This period saw the advent of railroads and the use of wicker for passenger car seats, and wicker seats graced the lounges of many transatlantic steamers.

Armchair

Baby carriage

Bentwood: 1870-1930

As we have implied, new design is often a reaction against an earlier style. It can also be imported from abroad. The Bentwood chair, immensely popular today, had its origin in Austria in the 1840s where it was designed and manufactured by Michael Thonet. Curved pieces of beech wood, stained in dark tones to suggest more expensive mahogany or rosewood, were imported from Europe and assembled in this country. The absence of hand-carved joints and decoration made it possible to put a piece together with ten screws or less. By the end of the century, the chair was being imitated everywhere. Its plain curved line and simplicity of form was appealing; it shared a place in the American home with the 19th-century revivals.

Bentwood furniture

Art Nouveau: 1895-1915

Art Nouveau, a style more frequently expressed in glass created by Louis Comfort Tiffany than in furniture, employed naturalistic designs of plants, flowers, leaves and tendrils. There were relatively few pieces of furniture of this style made in America; furniture made in Europe, especially in Britain by Mackintosh, Voysey and Mackmurdo, is better known.

The Arts and Crafts Movement: 1880-1915

Designers at the end of the 19th century were, above all, reformers, working to reunite art and craftsmanship which they felt had been tragically lost after about 1830. William Morris and John Ruskin had formed the basic philosophy for the Arts and Crafts movement in England; several American designers, influenced by their ideas, sought to return to the handcrafted object. Many felt, and still do today, that the Industrial Revolution, with all of its marvelous machines capable of creating the furniture of the Rococo Revival, stifled the role of the individual craftsman.

Mission Style: 1890-1915

In about 1900 Gustav Stickley, one of the first to comprehend the English proponents of the Arts and Crafts movement, began producing some of America's most functional furniture. Stickley, working in oak, created pieces of great linear strength. High slat backs on chairs were popular; joints were not disguised; metal and leather were sometimes used in small decorative spaces. Upholstering was done in canvas and leather. Stickley's designs were produced in Grand Rapids and widely imitated, particularly by Elbert Hubbard and his "Roycrafters."

By 1915 the intense competition from imitators, together with a decline in popularity of Mission Style furniture as taste swung to a new colonial revival, had forced Stickley into bankruptcy.

Mission furniture,
Gustav Stickley

Prairie School: 1895-1915

In tracing furniture history, we tend to emphasize those examples which set a trend, define a style, or evoke a new era. The designers of such furniture, while influential, produced relatively few pieces and these were well beyond the means of the average American.

Just such an innovative designer was Frank Lloyd Wright, best known for his Prairie School of architecture. He first built furniture for his own use and later for his "prairie houses." Wright designed furniture to replicate and harmonize with the exterior structure of his buildings. His chairs, often done in oak and very linear in style with high, straight backs, showed an Oriental influence.

By 1890 Chicago had surpassed New York in furniture making and Wright was able to commission craftsmen in small cabinetshops, there and in Milwaukee, to execute his furniture designs. Wright's major design statement for furniture consisted of his painted metal rectilinear office chairs and desks for the Larkin Office Building in Buffalo, New York. Ever since Wright's entry into office furniture in 1904, designers and craftsmen have devoted increased attention to the office as a designed space.

Unlike other Arts and Crafts designers, Wright made effective use of the machine. Devoted to function and clear line, he remains one of the most significant precursors of 20th-century design.

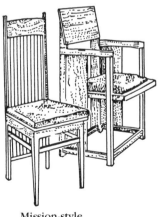

Mission-style
side chair,
Frank Lloyd Wright.
ca. 1895

Armchair and side chair,
Frank Lloyd Wright. 1904

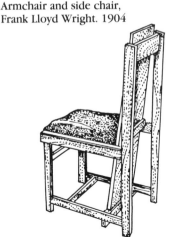

Art Deco: 1918-1939

This major style, Art Deco or "art moderne," flourished between World War I and World War II. It was influenced by the designers of the Bauhaus school, as well as Le Corbusier, Rietveld and Frank Lloyd Wright. Interest in machines was reflected in machine-like forms and mechanized production.

The term "Art Deco" derives from the name of the first major international exhibition of decorative arts, held in Paris in 1925, L'Exposition Internationale des Arts Décoratifs et Industriels Modernes. Elements of the Art Deco style were reflected in the ceramics, glass and silverware of this period.

Furniture designers used chrome and plastic; zig zags, circles and geometric patterns were incorporated; designs were "streamlined" like Raymond Loewy's designs for train engines. Art Deco triumphed in Donald Deskey's designs for the interior and furnishings of Radio City Music Hall. Furniture made by Emile-Jacques Ruhlmann, Eliel Saarinen and Eugene Schoen illustrate this style.

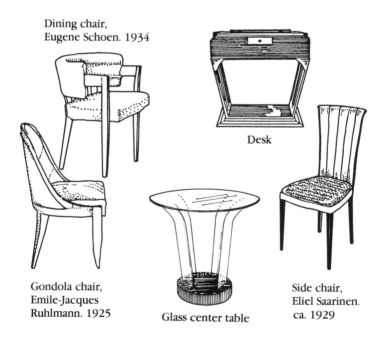

Dining chair, Eugene Schoen. 1934

Desk

Gondola chair, Emile-Jacques Ruhlmann. 1925

Glass center table

Side chair, Eliel Saarinen. ca. 1929

In large measure this style comes to us from a group of designers and architects trained in Europe. Their designs, many of them developed for design firms Knoll International and Herman Miller, combine form and function in styles that have endured despite the vogue for change. While many of the designers whose work we illustrate in this section are not Americans, their designs have affected nearly every facet of the American furniture industry.

These designers have taken full advantage of new materials: plastics and plastic laminates, foam rubber, tubular steel, aluminum, molded plywood, chrome, Fiberglas, steel rod, Masonite, vinyl, sheet metal, polyester and, more recently, poured concrete. A style was created which could be effectively reproduced for a large market.

As we approach the end of the 20th century, design innovations are coming quickly from a variety of sources. Memphis, the Milan-based, avant garde design movement, has produced adventurous experiments. Major designs, particularly in Japanese textiles, are coming from the Orient. These influences can be seen in the work exhibited at Westweek, a furniture market and conference held annually in West Hollywood, California. In general, the furniture tends to be comfortable, uncomplicated, and grand in scale. The textures of both the structures and textiles are natural, and some handcrafting is evident.

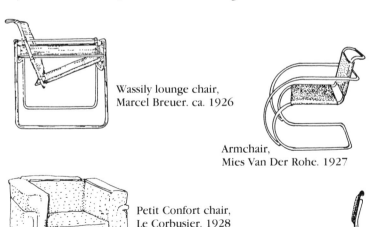

Wassily lounge chair,
Marcel Breuer. ca. 1926

Armchair,
Mies Van Der Rohe. 1927

Petit Confort chair,
Le Corbusier. 1928

Cesca side chair,
Marcel Breuer. 1928

Barcelona chair,
Mies Van Der Rohe. 1929

Lounge chair,
Alvar Aalto. 1934

Butterfly chair,
Harry Bertoia.
1938

Side chairs,
Charles and Ray Eames. ca. 1946

Armchair,
Charles and Ray Eames. 1949

"Round" chair,
Hans J. Wegner. 1949

Armchair and ottoman,
Eero Saarinen. 1948

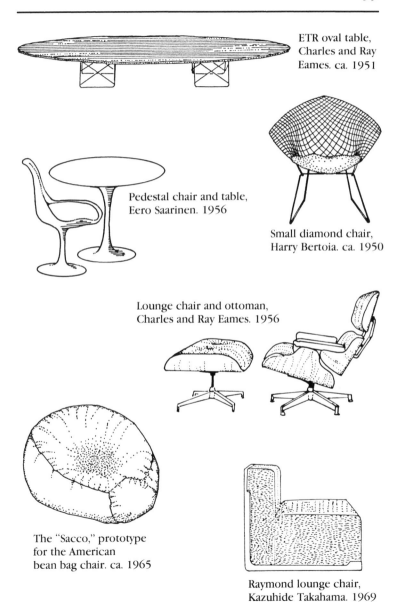

ETR oval table,
Charles and Ray
Eames. ca. 1951

Pedestal chair and table,
Eero Saarinen. 1956

Small diamond chair,
Harry Bertoia. ca. 1950

Lounge chair and ottoman,
Charles and Ray Eames. 1956

The "Sacco," prototype
for the American
bean bag chair. ca. 1965

Raymond lounge chair,
Kazuhide Takahama. 1969

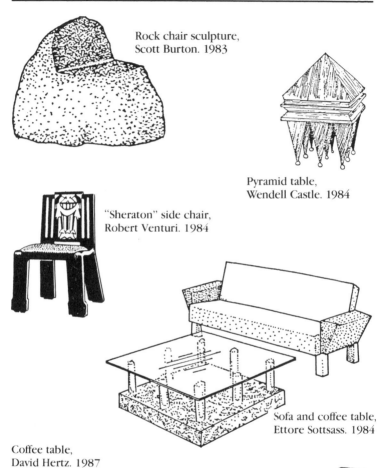

Rock chair sculpture,
Scott Burton. 1983

Pyramid table,
Wendell Castle. 1984

"Sheraton" side chair,
Robert Venturi. 1984

Sofa and coffee table,
Ettore Sottsass. 1984

Coffee table,
David Hertz. 1987

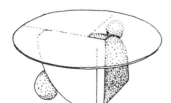

Mandarin chair,
Ettore Sottsass. 1987

Individual artists and craftsmen, whose innovative hand-crafted pieces are not only sculptural works of art but functional as well, are contributing significantly to 20th-century furniture design.

A variety of craft schools are now graduating furniture craftsmen and artisans. Programs in furniture and woodworking are offered at the Cooper Union, the Rhode Island School of Design, the Corcoran School of Art, the Cranbrook Academy of Art, the North Bennet Street School (Boston), the Parsons School of Design, and the Wendell Castle School, Rochester Institute of Technology.

The work of craftsmen and women can be located through such organizations as the Washington Woodworkers Guild or the Boston University Program in Artisanry. It is often shown in fine arts galleries.

Sam Maloof, working in California, creates handsome seating furniture somewhat reminiscent of 19th-century Windsor pieces. The woods are selected for color and graining and then carefully sculpted.

Rocking chair,
Sam Maloof. 1959

George Nakashima, Bucks County, Pennsylvania, was trained as an architect but became disenchanted with the execution of modern buildings which seemed to glorify the machine and cast aside the individual craftsman. He found that knowledge of structural engineering was as critical to the design of a chair as to the design of a house.

Nakashima works only in solid wood and maintains that the wood itself dictates the form and shape of each individual piece of furniture. The Conoid chair combines handcraftsmanship (in forming the frame and the seat) with a small amount of machine technology (in preparing the spindles). Since Nakashima's death in 1990, his daughter is carrying on his work.

Conoid table and chairs,
George Nakashima. 1962

Peter Danko, working near Washington, DC, skillfully combines fine
craftsmanship and design in the production of solid bent plywood
furniture characterized by graceful curves and natural forms. A
one-piece chair, shaped by Danko from
a single piece of plywood, has earned
a place in the Museum of Modern Art.

Bodyform chair,
Peter Danko. 1990

Peter Danko says, "all my chairs should remind people of something other than a chair." His latest designs are "organic shapes." Using the bentwood process allows the chair to be both lighter and stronger.

Side chair, table and sofa, Peter Danko. ca. 1980

Side table, Robert Trotman. 1987

Robert Trotman, an artist working in North Carolina, designs furniture which incorporates human arms and legs. Trotman's pieces, like those of the other craftsmen discussed here, can be found in museums and other collections of fine arts.

Recent artists/craftsmen who follow Nakashima and Maloof were termed the "second generation of studio furniture-makers," at an exhibition organized by Edward S. Cooke, Jr. of the Boston Museum of Fine Arts. This group studied or taught together during the 1970s and 1980s at the Rhode Island School of Design, the Rochester Institute of Technology's School for American Craftsmen, and Boston University's Program in Artisanry. They include Kristina Madsen, Richard Scott Newman, John Hunnigan, Thomas Hucker, Wendy Staymon and Rick Wrigley, Judy Kensley McKie and John Cederquist.

Women are becoming increasingly more involved in furniture making.

Leopard Chest,
Judy Kensley McKie. 1989

Hat rack,
Wendy Maruyama. 1987

Additional examples of "art furniture" or "new wave furniture" are shown. *Metropolis* magazine terms these examples "furniture for a new age." The 1980s produced a new generation of designer-architect artisans and craftspeople all working individually, almost in isolation. The first International Contemporary Furniture Fair in America, held recently in New York, gave 118 of these innovative designers an opportunity to show new work.

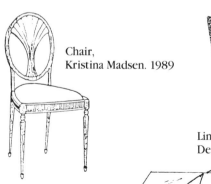

Chair,
Kristina Madsen. 1989

Cities table,
Al Glass. 1990

Lin table,
Demir Hamani. 1990

California:

    Los Angeles County Museum of Art, Los Angeles (furniture of
       the 18th and 19th centuries)
    Southwest Museum, Los Angeles (19th)
    Oakland Museum, Oakland (19th)
    M.H. De Young Museum, San Francisco (18th, 19th)

Colorado:

    State Historical Society of Colorado, Denver and other locations
       in the State (19th)

Connecticut:

    Connecticut Historical Society, Hartford (17th, 18th, 19th)
    Mark Twain Memorial, Hartford (19th)
    Wadsworth Athenaeum, Hartford (17th, 18th)
    New Haven Colony Historical Society, New Haven (17th)
    Yale University Art Gallery, New Haven (17th, 18th, 19th, 20th)
    The Webb-Deane Stevens Museum, Wethersfield (17th)

Delaware:

    Historical Society of Delaware, Wilmington and New Castle
       (18th, 19th)
    Rockwood Museum, Wilmington (19th)
    Winterthur Museum, Winterthur (17th, 18th, 19th)

District of Columbia:

    Daughters of the American Revolution Museum (17th, 18th, 19th)
    Diplomatic Reception Rooms, U.S.Department of State (18th, 19th)
    National Museum of American History, Smithsonian Institute
       (17th, 18th, 19th, 20th)
    The Octagon (19th)
    Renwick Gallery, Smithsonian Institution (20th c. exhibitions)
    Tudor Place (19th)
    The White House (18th, 19th)

Florida:

    Henry Morrison Flagler Museum, Palm Beach (19th)
    Historic Pensacola Preservation Board, Pensacola (19th)
    Lightner Museum, Saint Augustine (19th)

Georgia:

    Atlanta Historical Society, Atlanta (19th)
    High Museum of Art, Atlanta (18th, 19th)
    Telfair Academy of Arts and Sciences, Savannah (18th, 19th)

Illinois:

    The Art Institute, Chicago (18th, 19th, 20th)

    Chicago Historical Society, Chicago (19th, 20th)

    Frank Lloyd Wright Home and Studio, Oak Park (20th)

Indiana:

    Indianapolis Museum of Art, Indianapolis (18th, 19th)

    President Benjamin Harrison Memorial Home, Indianapolis (19th)

Kentucky:

    Shakertown at Pleasant Hill (19th)

Louisiana:

    Anglo-American Art Museum, Baton Rouge (18th, 19th)

    Gallier House, New Orleans (19th)

Maine:

    United Society of Shakers, Sabbathday Lake, Poland Springs (19th)

    Maine Historical Society, Portland (18th, 19th)

    Portland Museum of Art, Portland (18th, 19th)

Maryland:

    Historic Annapolis Foundation, Annapolis (18th, 19th)

    Baltimore Museum of Art, Baltimore (18th, 19th)

    Homewood Museum, Baltimore (19th)

    Maryland Historical Society, Baltimore (18th, 19th)

    Hampton National Historic Site, Towson (18th, 19th)

Massachusetts:

    Museum of Fine Arts, Boston (17th, 18th, 19th, 20th)

    Society for the Preservation of New England Antiquities,
      Boston and other places throughout New England (17th, 18th, 19th)

    Historic Deerfield, Inc., Deerfield (18th)

    Hancock Shaker Village, Pittsfield (18th)

    Essex Institute, Salem (17th, 18th, 19th)

    Old Sturbridge Village, Sturbridge (18th, 19th)

    Sterling and Francine Clark Art Institute, Williamstown (18th)

    Worcester Art Museum, Worcester (18th)

Michigan:

    Cranbrook Academy, Bloomfield Hills (20th)

    Greenfield Village and Henry Ford Museum, Dearborn (17th, 18th, 19th)

    Detroit Historical Museum, Detroit (19th)

    Grand Rapids Public Museum, Grand Rapids (19th, 20th)

Minnesota:
Minneapolis Institute of Arts, Minneapolis (18th, 19th, 20th)

Mississippi:
Rosalie, Natchez (19th)

Missouri:
Saint Louis Art Museum, St. Louis (17th, 18th, 19th, 20th)

New Hampshire:
The Museum at Lower Shaker Village, Enfield, (19th)
Currier Gallery of Art, Manchester (17th, 18th)
Strawbery Banke, Portsmouth (18th, 19th)

New Jersey:
Ballantine House, Newark (19th)
New Jersey State Museum, Trenton (18th)

New Mexico:
Museum of New Mexico, Santa Fe (19th)

New York:
Brooklyn Museum, Brooklyn (17th, 18th, 19th)
Boscobel, Garrison-on-the-Hudson (19th)
Cooper-Hewitt Museum of Design, New York (20th)
Metropolitan Museum, New York (17th, 18th, 19th, 20th)
Museum of Modern Art, New York (20th)
New-York Historical Society, New York (18th, 19th)
Shaker Museum, Old Chatham (19th)
Strong Museum, Rochester (19th)
Lyndhurst, Tarrytown (19th)
Historic Hudson Valley, Inc., Tarrytown (18th)
Hudson River Museum, Yonkers (19th)

North Carolina:
Tryon Palace Restoration Complex, New Bern (18th)
Museum of Early Southern Decorative Arts, Winston-Salem
(17th, 18th, 19th)

Ohio:
Cincinnati Art Museum, Cincinnati (19th)
Western Reserve Historical Society, Cleveland (18th, 19th)
Toledo Museum of Art, Toledo (18th)

Oregon:
Oregon Historical Society, Portland (19th)

Pennsylvania:

    Philadelphia Museum of Art, Philadelphia (18th, 19th)
    Carnegie Institute, Pittsburgh (18th, 19th)
    Chester County Historical Society, West Chester (17th, 18th, 19th)
    York County Historical Society, York (18th)

Rhode Island:

    Museum of Art, Rhode Island School of Design, Providence (18th)

South Carolina:

    Historic Charleston Foundation, Charleston (18th, 19th)

Texas:

    Dallas Museum of Art, Dallas (18th, 19th)
    Ashton Villa, Galveston (19th)
    Bayou Bend, Houston (17th, 18th, 19th, 20th)
    Harris County Heritage Society, Houston (19th, 20th)
    Winedale, Round Top (19th)
    San Antonio Museum of Art, San Antonio (18th, 19th)

Vermont:

    Shelburne Museum, Shelburne (18th, 19th)

Virginia:

    Virginia Museum of Fine Arts, Richmond (18th, 19th, 20th)
    Stratford Hall, Stratford (18th)
    Abby Aldrich Rockefeller Folk Art Center, Williamsburg (19th)
    DeWitt Wallace Collection, Colonial Williamsburg (17th, 18th)

Wisconsin:

    Milwaukee Art Museum, Milwaukee (18th, 19th)

Bishop, Robert. *The American Chair: Three Centuries of Style*. New York: Dutton, 1972.

Burton, E. Milby. *Charleston Furniture, 1700-1825*. Columbia, SC: University of South Carolina Press, 1970.

Fairbanks, Jonathan et al. *New England Begins*. Boston: Museum of Fine Arts, 1982.

Garvan, Beatrice B. *Federal Philadelphia, 1785-1825*. Philadelphia: Philadelphia Museum of Art, 1987.

Jobe, Brock and Myrna Kaye. *New England Furniture: The Colonial Era*. Boston: Houghton Mifflin Company, 1984.

Kane, Patricia E. *Furniture of the New Haven Colony: The Seventeenth-Century Style*. New Haven Colony Historical Society, 1973.

Kirk, John T. *American Chairs: Queen Anne and Chippendale*. New York: Alfred A. Knopf, 1972.

_____ . *American Furniture and the British Tradition to 1830*. New York: Alfred A. Knopf, 1982.

Montgomery, Charles F. *American Furniture: The Federal Period*. New York: Bonanza Books, 1978.

Morse, John D., ed. *Country Cabinetwork and Simple City Furniture*. Winterthur Conference Report, 1969.

Puig, Francis and Michael Conforti, eds. *The American Craftsman and the European Tradition, 1620-1820*. Hanover, NH and London: University Press of New England, 1989.

Quimby, Ian M. G., ed. *The Craftsman in Early America*. New York: W. W. Norton and Company, 1984.

Steinfeldt, Cecilia and Donald Lewis Stover. *Early Texas Furniture and Decorative Arts*. San Antonio: Trinity University Press, 1973.

Weidman, Gregory. *Furniture in Maryland, 1740-1940*. Baltimore: Maryland Historical Society, 1984.

Aalto, Alvar, *58*
Acanthus-leaf carving, *25*
Ackermann, Rudolph, 37
Adam brothers, 32
African design, 44
Art Deco style, 56
Art Moderne. *See* Art Deco style
Art Nouveau style, 53
Artists/Craftsmen, 61-64
Arts and Crafts Movement, 54

Baroque (Queen Anne) style, 16-21
Baudouine, Charles, 49
Bauhaus school, 56
Belter, John Henry, 49
Bentwood style, 53
Bertoia, Harry, *58, 59*
Biedermeier style, 44
Bird-cage support, *20*
Block-front, 25, *28*
Bombé, 25, *28*
Bonnet top, *21, 29*
Breuer, Marcel, 57
Burton, Scott, *60*

Cartouche, *24,* 50
Castle, Wendell, *60*
Chairs: bannister-back, *14;*
    Barcelona, 58; bean bag, *59;*
    Bodyform, *62;* Butterfly, *58;* Cesca,
    57; comb-back, *46;* Conoid, *62;*
    Cromwellian, *11;* diamond, *59;*
    "fancy," 43, *46;* gondola, *56;*
    Hitchcock, 43, *46;* hoop-back, *46;*
    klismos-type, *40;* ladder-back, *45;*
    lyre-back, *40;* Mandarin, *60;* pedestal,
    59; Petit Confort, *57;* plank, *47;*
    Raymond lounge, *59;* rock sculpture,
    60; "Round," *58;* rustic
    (Adirondack), *45;* shield-back, *31,
    33;* wainscot, 9, *11;* Wassily lounge,
    57; windsor, 43, *46*
Chests: blanket, *15;*
    chest-on-chest, *26;* chest-on-frame,
    15, 19, 29; dower, 9, *11;* high, 18, *20,
    21, 29;* low (dressing tables), *19, 27*

Chinoiserie, *17*
Chippendale, Thomas, 23
Chippendale style. *See* Rococo
Clock, case, *26*
Colonial revival, 51
Country furniture, 42-47
Craftsmen. *See* Artists/Craftsmen
Crest rails, *17, 23*
Crown-and-claws, 24
Cupboards: armoire, *47;*
    chimney, *46;* corner, *44;* court, *10;*
    jelly, *45;* pie safe, *44;* schrank, *43, 47*

Danko, Peter, 62-63, *62, 63*
Davenport, A. H., 51
Day-bed, *15*
Deskey, Donald, 56
Desks: desk-on-frame, *20;* slant-top,
    29; and bookcase, *34;* tambourrout,
    35; secrétaire à abattant 39
Downing, Andrew Jackson, 48
Drawer pulls: *13, 17, 24, 31*

Eames, Charles and Ray, *58, 59*
Eastlake, Charles, 50
Eastlake style, 50-51
Eglomisé, *31, 32, 35*
Empire. *See* Neoclassical II
Etagère, 49

Federal. *See* Neoclassical I
Foot: ball-and-claw, 18, *25;*
    straight bracket, *25;* bun, *13;*
    C-scroll, *37;* ogee bracket, *25;* pad,
    18; paw, *37;* Roman, *38;* slipper, *18;*
    spade, *32;* Spanish, *13;* trifid, *18*
Finial, *24*
Folk furniture, 42-47
Fontaine, P. F. L., 37
French colonial style, 44, 47
Fretwork, Chinese, *23*

Gadrooning, *23*
Girandole, *39*
Glass, Al, *64*
Gothic revival, 48

Grand Rapids, 51, 54

Hamani, Demir, *64*
Hepplewhite, George, 32
Herter, Christian, 50-51
Hertz, David, *60*
Hitchcock, Lambert, 43
Hope, Thomas, 32
Hubbard, Elbert, 54

Inlay, 31; bellflower, 31, *32;*
    eagle, *32;* fan, *32;* paterae, *32*
International style, 57-60

Jacobean style, 9-10
Japanning, 17
Joints: butt, *9;* dove-tail,
    9; mortise-and-tenon, *9*
Joint stool, *10*

Knoll International, 57

Lannuier, Charles Honoré, 37, 44
Larkin Office Building, 55
Le Corbusier, 56, 57
Leg: cabriole, 17, *18;*
    klismos, 38, *40;* Marlborough, *25;*
    reeded, *32;* spade, *32;* straight, *25,*
    vase-and-rumpet, *13*

Madsen, Kristina, 63, *64*
Maloof, Sam, 61, *61*
Mannerist style, 10
Marcotte, Leon, 50
Marquetry, 50
Maruyama, Wendy, *64*
McIntire, Samuel, *41*
McKie, Judy Kensley, 63, *64*
Meeks, Joseph, and Sons, 49
Memphis movement, 57
Méridienne, 49
Miller, Herman, 57
Mission style, 54
Morris, William, 54

Nakashima, George, 61, *62*

Neoclassical I, 30-35
Neoclassical II, 36-41

Ormulu, 50

Pabst, Daniel, 51
Pennsylvania Germans, 43
Percier, Charles, 37
Phyfe, Duncan, 38
Pierced bannister, 24
Pilgrim. *See* 17th century.
Pompeiian red, 38
Prairie School, 55
Prince of Wales feathers, *38*

Quarter column, *23*
Queen Anne. *See* Baroque

Radio City Music Hall, 56
Renaissance revival, 50
Rietveld, 56
Rococo (Chippendale) style, 22-29
Rococo revival, 49
Rosette, *24*
Roux, Alexander, 49
Roycrafters, 54
Ruhlmann, Emile-Jacques, 56
Ruskin, John, 54

Saarinen, Eero, *58, 59*
Saarinen, Eliel, *56*
Schoen, Eugene, *56*
Scott, Sir Walter, 48
Serpentine-front, *28, 34*
17th-century furniture, 8-11
Shaker furniture, 43, *46*
Shearer, Thomas, 32
Shell carving, *18, 24*
Sheraton, Thomas, 32
Sottsass, Ettore, *60*
Spanish colonial, 44, *47*
Splats: urn-shaped, *33;* vase, *17*
Split spindles, *9*
Stickley, Gustav, 54, *54*
Stop fluting, *25*

Tables: candle stands, *27, 34;*
    card, *21, 29, 35, 39, 40;* dressing, *15,*
    19, 29; drop-leaf, *21, 46;* ETR oval,
    59; gateleg, *14;* lady's work, *33, 41;*
    pembroke, *28;* pier, 38, *39;* tea, *20,*
    21, 26; tilt-top, *20*
Takahama, Kazuhide, *59*
Thonet, Michael, 53
Tiffany, Louis Comfort, 53
Trotman, Robert, 62, *62*

Van Der Rohe, Mies, *57, 58*

Veneer, *32*
Venturi, Robert, *60*
Victorian styles, 48-51
Vitruvius, 18

Wegner, Hans J., *58*
Water-leaf carving, *37*
Westweek, 57
Wicker furniture, 52
William and Mary style, 12-15
Wright, Frank Lloyd, 55, *55,* 56